Challenge
Copying Masters

Grade 1

Harcourt School Publishers

www.harcourtschool.com

Printed in the United States of America

ISBN 10: 0-15-349890-0
ISBN 13: 978-0-15-349890-9

5 6 7 8 9 10 054 17 16 14 13 12 11 10 09 08

Contents

Challenge
© Harcourt • Grade 1

Spring Forward

Book 1-1

▶ **Circle the sentence that tells about the picture.**

1.

We have a map.

We have a cat.

2.

Pam has a van.

Pam has a hat.

3.

Pat ran to me.

Pat sat down.

4.

She has a can.

She has a bag.

5.

We can nap.

We can tap.

School–Home Connection

Have your child read each sentence aloud.
Ask which words have the short *a* sound as
in *cat*.

2

▶ **Write a word from the box to complete each sentence.**

| ran | nap | hat | sat | sad | tan |

_____
- - - - - - - - - - -
1. Dad _____ down.

_____
- - - - - - - - -
2. Jan has a _____ .

_____
- - - - - - - - -
3. Max had a _____ .

✎ **Try This**

Choose a word from the box. Write a sentence of
your own.

 School–Home Connection

Have your child read each sentence. Then have
your child make up more sentences using the
words in the box.

4

Name _____

▶ **Write a word from the box to complete each sentence.**

| help | Now | Let's |

_____
----

1. _____ we have to go.

_____

_____
----

2. A map can _____ .

_____

_____
----

3. _____ go.

🖊 **Try This**

Write another sentence using a word from the box.

🚒 **School–Home Connection**

Have your child read each sentence aloud. Encourage your child to use the words in the box to write other sentences.

5

Challenge
© Harcourt • Grade 1 • Book 1

Name _____

▶ **Look at the picture. Write a sentence that tells what will probably happen next.**

1.

_____
- - - - - - - - - - - - - -
_____
- - - - - - - - - - - - - -
_____

2.

_____
- - - - - - - - - - - - - -
_____
- - - - - - - - - - - - - -
_____

3.

_____
- - - - - - - - - - - - - -
_____
- - - - - - - - - - - - - -
_____

✎ **Try This**

Choose one sentence. Draw a picture.

School–Home Connection

Have your child read aloud a sentence. Then ask *"What clues helped you predict what would probably happen next?"*

6

▶ **Add s to each word. Write the new word in the sentence.**

pat
_____
- - - - - - - - - - - - - - - - - -

1. Max _____ the cat.

_____

tag
_____
- - - - - - - - - - - - - - - - - -

2. Sam _____ Dan.

_____

nap
_____
- - - - - - - - - - - - - - - - - -

3. I like _____.

_____

map
_____
- - - - - - - - - - - - - - - - - - - -

4. We have two _____.

_____

bat
_____
- - - - - - - - - - - - - - - - - -

5. Jan _____.

School–Home Connection

Have your child think of other words and add s to them. Ask him or her to say the words in a sentence.

Challenge

► **Write a word from the box to complete each sentence.**

mad	ran	cat	pan	can	wag

_____
- - - - - - - - - - - - - - - - - - -

1. I see a _____ .

_____
- - - - - - - - - - - - - - - - - - -

2. Pat has a _____ .

_____
- - - - - - - - - - - - - - - - - - -

3. Jan _____ out.

_____
- - - - - - - - - - - - - - - - - - -

4. I am _____ .

🖊 **Try This**

Choose a word from the box. Write a sentence of your own.

School–Home Connection

Have your child read each sentence aloud. Then have your child say more sentences using the words in the box.

Challenge

▶ **Use the mixed-up letters to write words.**
Use two of the words in the sentences.
Draw a picture for each sentence.

n a t p		
m a p d		

_____
- - - - - - - - - - - - - - - -

1. Max has a _____.

_____
- - - - - - - - - - - - - - - -

2. I see a _____.

School–Home Connection

Write the words *map* and *ran.* Then ask your
child to say a sentence that uses both words.

11

▶ **Write a word from the box to complete each sentence.**

in	too	no

1. Dad had a cap _____ the bag.

2. I had _____ cap.

3. Now I have a cap, _____.

🚒 **School–Home Connection**

Have your child read each sentence aloud. Help
your child think of a sentence using two words
from the box.

Challenge

Name _____

▶ **Read each story. Look at the picture.
Write a sentence that tells what will
happen next.**

1. Dad and Sam like ham.
They want to have ham now.
There is ham in the pan.

_____

- -

_____

_____

2. Jan is sad. She had a bag.
Now, she has no bag. Dad
can see the bag. The bag is
in the van.

_____

- -

_____

 Try This

Think about the story, "Sad, Sad Dan." Make a prediction
about what might happen next. Draw a picture.

 **School–Home Connection**

Tell a favorite story to your child. As you tell
the story, pause and ask your child to predict
what might happen next.

Challenge
© Harcourt • Grade 1 • Book 1

▶ **Add letters to ag and and to make
words. Write the words in the box.**

b   s   n

j   t   h

r   w   l

___ **ag**

___ **and**

School–Home Connection

Ask your child to say some of the words he or
she made in sentences. Encourage your child to
write one sentence using one of the words.

Challenge
© Harcourt • Grade 1 • Book 1

Name _____

▶ **Circle the sentence that tells about
the picture.**

1. Kim will give a gift.

   Kim will sit and dig.

2. It will miss the bin.

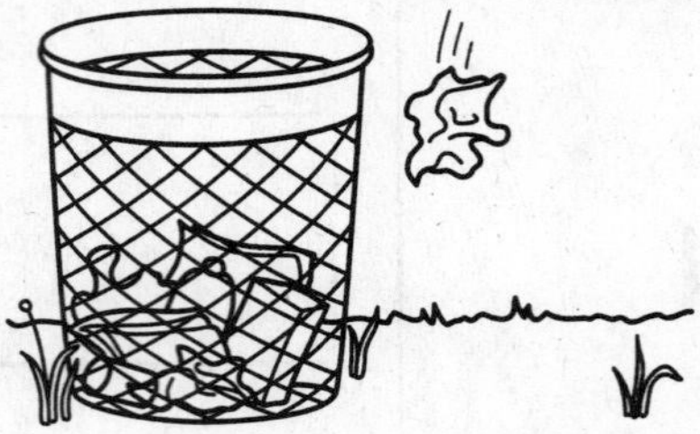

   It will miss the ban.

3. Tim has six pigs.

   Tim has to lift pins.

4. Jim will give him a mat.

   Jim will give him a mitt.

5. Liz sat to sip the milk.

   Liz sits in the mist.

School–Home Connection

Have your child read each sentence aloud.
Ask him or her to choose a sentence that is not
circled and then draw a picture for it.

16

Name _____

▶ **Use the letters to make words. Then
use the words to complete the sentences.
Draw a picture for each sentence.**

p d r g i		
h t m l i		

_____

- - - - - - - - - - - - - -

1. I have a _____ .

_____

- - - - - - - - - - - - - -

2. I can _____ .

School–Home Connection

Write the words *wind* and *gift*. Have your child
read each word and say it in a sentence.

18

Challenge

▶ **Write the word that best completes the sentence.**

| so | hold | get | home | soon |

_____

- - - - - - - - - - - - - - - - - -

1. Dad will get here _____ .

_____

_____

- - - - - - - - - - - - - - - - - -

2. Now Dad has come _____ .

_____

_____

- - - - - - - - - - - - - - - - - -

3. I ran _____ fast to Dad.

_____

_____

- - - - - - - - - - - - - - - - - -

4. I will _____ milk for Dad.

_____

_____

- - - - - - - - - - - - - - - - - -

5. He will _____ me in his lap.

Try This

Write a new sentence with one of the words. Draw a picture to go with your sentence.

School–Home Connection

Have your child read each sentence aloud.
Then point to each word your child wrote.
Have your child read each word, close his or
her eyes, and then spell the word.

19

Challenge
© Harcourt • Grade 1 • Book 1

Name _____

▶ **Trace the words Animals and Things.**
Then write words from the box in the
group where they belong.

ant	cat	mask	van
pig	cap	lamp	ram

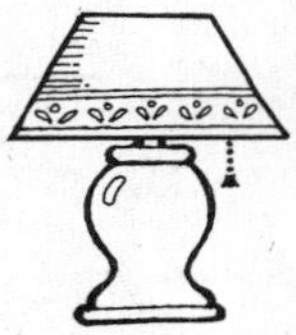

Animals | Things

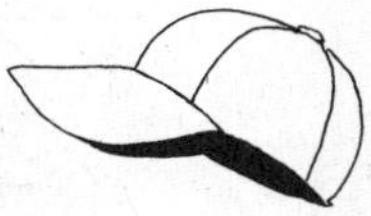

 Try This

Write a sentence that tells about one of the animals and
one of the things.

🚒 **School–Home Connection**
Talk about how the things in each column are
alike. Ask your child to think of other things
that belong in each group and draw pictures.

20

Challenge
© Harcourt • Grade 1 • Book 1

Name _____

▶ **Write the word from the box that completes each sentence.**

It's	She's	He's
Here's	There's	What's

_____

----

1. Liz is at camp. _____ sad.

_____

----

2. _____ no cat at camp.

_____

----

3. _____ a gift for you.

_____

----

4. _____ this?

_____

----

5. _____ a cat mask!
It looks like my cat.

School–Home Connection

Have your child read each sentence aloud.
Ask him or her to tell what two words each
contraction stands for.

21

Challenge
© Harcourt • Grade 1 • Book 1

► **Look at each picture. Write the word in the box that completes the sentence.**

tick	pack	back	lick
sack	kick	pick	rack

_____

1. Kim sat in the _____.

_____

2. Pat lifts the _____.

_____

3. I _____ up the mat.

_____

4. I _____ it to Pam.

Try This

Write a sentence using another word from the box.

School–Home Connection

Have your child read the words in the box. Ask him or her to point to and say the words that rhyme.

23

► **Look at the picture clues. Then write the words where they belong in the puzzles.**

back	jacks	kick	lick
pack	pick	sack	sick

1.

2.

3.

4.

5.

6.

7.

8.

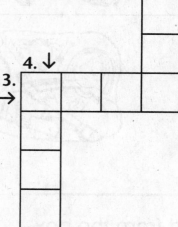

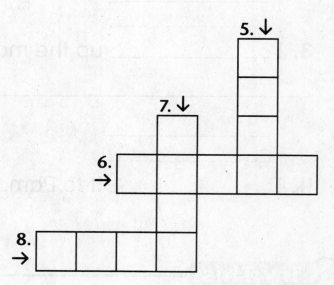

School–Home Connection

Have your child read aloud each word in the puzzle. Together, think of other words that end with *ck*.

Challenge

▶ **Write a word from the box to complete each sentence.**

Oh	late	Yes

_____
- - - - - - - - - - - - - - - -

1. We are _____! We will have to go soon.

_____

_____
- - - - - - - - - - - - - - - -

2. _____, Nick! Will you help me?

_____

_____
- - - - - - - - - - - - - - - -

3. _____, Dad, I will help. I will help get the bags to the van.

✎ **Try This**

Write a new sentence with one of the words.

 **School–Home Connection**

Have your child read each sentence aloud. Help your child read *Oh* and *Yes* with expression.

Challenge

Name _____

▶ **Write 1, 2, or 3 to put the pictures in story order. Then write sentences to tell the story.**

_____   _____   _____
- - - - - - - - - - - -   - - - - - - - - - - - -   - - - - - - - - - - - -
_____   _____   _____

_____
- -

1. _____

_____
- -

2. _____

_____
- -

3. _____

🖊 **Try This**

Draw a picture to show how the story ends.

School–Home Connection

Have your child tell what is happening in each picture. Then ask him or her to read aloud the sentences he or she wrote.

27

▶ **Circle the sentence that tells about the picture.**

1. Nick ran up a hill.
Nick ran to the pit.

2. Liz will dig in the sand pit.
Liz and Bill will sit.

3. Jill hit it and ran.
Yes, it will fit.

4. Jack will fit the mask.
Jack will fix the mill.

5. The ant bit the fig.
The ant is ill.

School–Home Connection

Have your child read each sentence aloud.
Ask him or her to draw a picture for a sentence
that is not circled.

28

Challenge

▶ **Read each sentence. Circle the word in each sentence that has the short o vowel sound. Write the word on the line.**

_____
----

1. Jim has a mop. _____

_____

_____
----

2. Sid got a mask as a gift. _____

_____

_____
----

3. Pat jogs past a ramp. _____

_____

_____
----

4. Bob has six caps. _____

_____

_____
----

5. His hat is big and soft. _____

_____

_____
----

6. Jan has two socks. _____

School–Home Connection

Ask your child to read aloud each sentence.
Together, think of a word that rhymes with the
word your child wrote.

30

Challenge
© Harcourt • Grade 1 • Book 1

Name _____

▶ **Use the letters to write words. Use two of the words in a sentence. Draw a picture for each sentence.**

m o t p		
h o g t n		

1. Sam has a _____ .

2. I see the _____ .

32

Challenge
© Harcourt • Grade 1 • Book 1

▶ **Choose the words that best complete the sentences. Write the words in the sentences and in the puzzle. You may use a word more than once.**

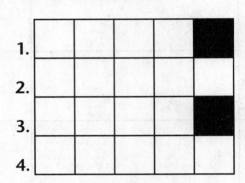

much
find
thank

_____
- - - - - - - - - - - - - - - -

1. It is hot. Jan will not dig _____.

_____
- - - - - - - - - - - - - - - -

2. Tom will help dig. Jan will _____ him.

_____
- - - - - - - - - - - - - - - -

3. Jill will help Sam _____ his hat.

_____
- - - - - - - - - - - - - - - -

4. Sam will _____ Jill.

School–Home Connection

Talk about an activity your child likes to do.
Help your child use the words in the box to
make up sentences about it.

33

▶ **Think of the story "Dot and Bob."**
Write the names of the characters and
draw pictures to tell about them.

Characters	Pictures

Try This

Write a sentence for each picture. Tell about the
character.

School–Home Connection

Talk about a story you have shared with your
child. Have your child name and describe a
character from that story.

Challenge
© Harcourt • Grade 1 • Book 1

▶ **Read each word in the box and each sentence. Add ed or ing to the word in the box. Write the new word to complete the sentence.**

1. ask   Tom _____ me to help.

2. camp   I like to go _____.

3. add   Pam _____ six and six.

4 fill   We have _____ up the box.

5. hand   Mom is _____ me a gift.

School–Home Connection

Have your child read aloud the completed
sentences. Together, think of other words and
add *-ed* and *-ing* to them.

Challenge
© Harcourt • Grade 1 • Book 1

▶ **Say the name of each picture. Then write the word. Each word ends with _all_.**

1. _____ _____ _____ _____

_____

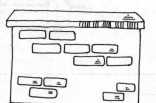

2. _____ _____ _____ _____

_____

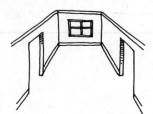

3. _____ _____ _____ _____

_____

4. _____ _____ _____ _____

_____

5. _____ _____ _____ _____

School–Home Connection

Ask your child to tell you how the words are
the same. Encourage him or her to write a
sentence using one of the words.

37

Challenge
© Harcourt • Grade 1 • Book 1

▶ **Write a word from the box to complete
the sentence.**

wall	ball	mall	call
tall	all	fall	hall

_____
- - - - - - - - - - - -

I. We are at the _____.

_____
- - - - - - - - - - - -

2. There is a map on the _____.

_____
- - - - - - - - - - - -

3. I got a _____ for Nick.

_____
- - - - - - - - - - - -

4. Mom got Nick a _____ hat.

_____
- - - - - - - - - - - -

5. Nick will like _____ the gifts.

✎ **Try This**

Choose a word from the box. Write your own sentence
for it.

🚒 **School–Home Connection**

Point to the words *call* and *hall*. Encourage
your child to write these words in other
sentences about Nick's family at the mall.

Challenge
© Harcourt • Grade 1 • Book 1

▶ **Write a word from the box to complete
the sentence.**

how	make	of	Some

_____

- - - - - - - - - - - - - - - -

1. Ann and Sam like to _____ masks.
_____

_____

- - - - - - - - - - - - - - - -

2. _____ masks are big.
_____

_____

- - - - - - - - - - - - - - - -

3. Ann has a bag _____ pink wigs, too.
_____

_____

- - - - - - - - - - - - - - - -

4. Mom asks _____ much the masks cost.

Try This

Write a new sentence with one of the words from the box.

School–Home Connection

Have your child read each completed sentence
aloud. Have him or her write a sentence about
something he or she likes to make.

40

▶ **Read the words in the box. Write two group names for the words. Then list the words in the group to which they belong.**

hop	kick	Bill	ran
Pam	Dan	jog	Rick

_____ | _____

_____ | _____

_____ | _____

_____ | _____

_____ | _____

_____ | _____

_____ | _____

_____ | _____

_____ | _____

 Try This

Use words from both groups to write sentences.

School–Home Connection

Talk about how the words in each group are the same. With your child, list other words that belong in each group.

41

Challenge

▶ **Write a contraction from the box to complete the sentence.**

can't	didn't	he's
isn't	She's	That's

_____

----

1. _____ my mom's van.

_____

_____

----

2. We _____ go in the van.

_____

_____

----

3. The van _____ fixed.

_____

_____

----

4. Mom _____ want to call a cab.

_____

_____

----

5. _____ going to see if Dad can fix it.

🚒 **School–Home Connection**

Have your child read each completed sentence aloud. Then have him or her tell you what two words make up the contraction.

Challenge
© Harcourt • Grade 1 • Book 1

Zoom Along

Book 1-2

▶ **Write the word from the box that completes each sentence.**

well	Ken	sell	help
best	pet	vet	pen

Jack and Ken

_____

Jack has a _____ dog. Jack calls the dog

_____   _____
------------------   ------------------

_____. Ken is the _____ pet.

_____

Ken is ill. Jack wants to _____. Jack gets

_____   _____
------------------   ------------------

him to the _____. Ken will get _____ now.

School–Home Connection
Have your child find words in the story with
the short *e* sound, as in *pet*.

2

Name _____

▶ **Use each set of letters to make four new words. Use two of the words to complete the sentences. Draw a picture for each sentence.**

b e t g p		
g e m l d n		

_____

----

1. Mom has a _____.

_____

----

2. I see the _____.

School–Home Connection

Write the words *beg* and *get*. Then ask your child to say a sentence that uses both words.

4

Challenge

© Harcourt • Grade 1 • Book 2

Name _____

▶ **Write a word from the box to complete each sentence.**

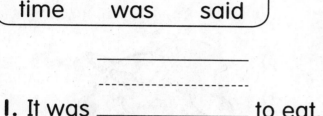

day	eat	first
time	was	said

1. It was _____ to eat.

2. Ann _____ she wanted to help.

3. Tim wanted to _____ eggs.

4. Tim _____ not helping.

5. Dad wanted Tim to help _____.

✎ **Try This**

Write a new sentence with one of the words from the box.

School–Home Connection

Have your child find *eat* and *day* in the box.
Ask your child to tell something he or she likes
to eat each day.

5

Challenge
© Harcourt • Grade 1 • Book 2

▶ **Look at the pictures. Write a sentence
telling how the animals are the same.
Write a sentence telling how they are different.**

1. _____
_____
_____
_____

2. _____
_____
_____

 **Try This**

Write a sentence that tells how a horse is the same as the
animals in the pictures.

School–Home Connection

Talk about how the animals in the pictures are
like and different from a pet you both know.

 6

Challenge
© Harcourt • Grade 1 • Book 2

Name _____

▶ **Draw lines to make words. Write the
words in the box.**

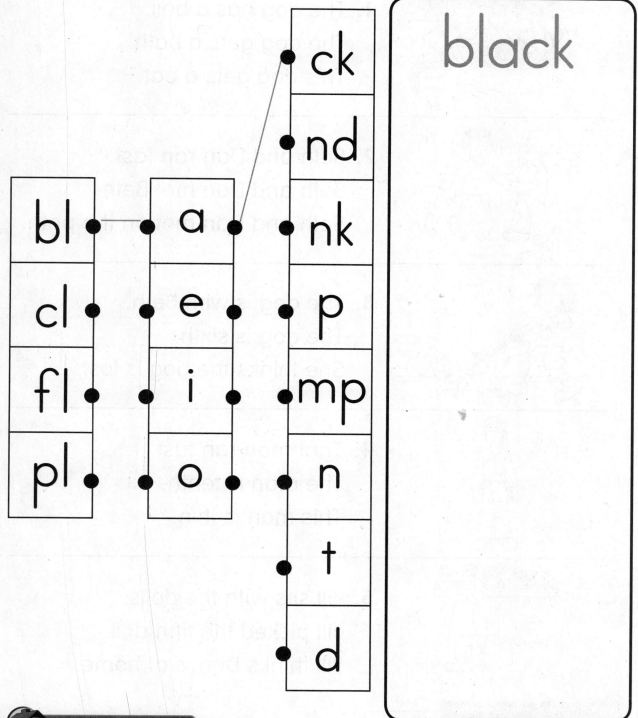

black

Challenge
© Harcourt • Grade 1 • Book 2

▶ **Circle the sentence that tells about each picture.**

1. The dog has a bell.

The dog gets a bath.

This dog gets a bat.

2. Seth and Dan ran fast.

Seth and Dan met Beth.

Seth and Dan met on the path.

3. The dog is with Beth.

The dog is sixth.

She thinks the dog is lost.

4. That man ran fast.

The man is tenth.

This man is thin.

5. Jill sits with the dolls.

Jill picked the fifth doll.

Jill thinks Don is at home.

School–Home Connection

Have your child read each sentence aloud. Together, think of other words that begin or end with *th*. Encourage your child to write each word in a sentence.

Challenge
© Harcourt • Grade 1 • Book 2

▶ **Write a word from the box to complete each sentence.**

sixth	Then	path	thank
this	think	That	Beth

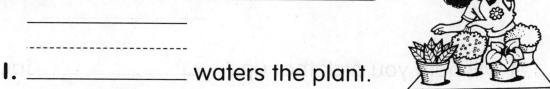

_____

----

1. _____ waters the plant.

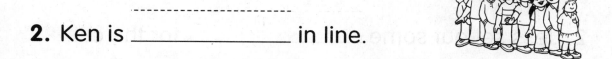

_____

----

2. Ken is _____ in line.

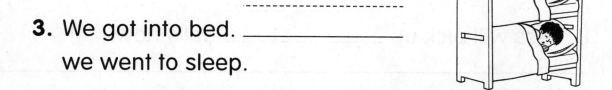

_____

----

3. We got into bed. _____ we went to sleep.

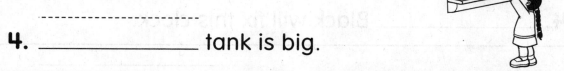

_____

----

4. _____ tank is big.

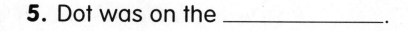

_____

----

5. Dot was on the _____ .

Try This

Write a sentence using one of the words from the box.

School–Home Connection

Have your child write a sentence using the words *thick* and *thin*.

11

Challenge

▶ **Write a word from the box to complete each sentence.**

| don't | her | line | Mr. |
| new | says | water | |

_____
- -

1. "I will help you pick that up," _____ Jack.

_____
- -

2. Jess set out some _____ for the cat.

_____
- -

3. Jess will pick up _____ dolls now.

_____
- - - - - - - - - - - - - - -

4. _____ Black will fix this clock.

_____
- -

5. Now we will not have to get a _____ clock.

 **Try This**

Write sentences using the words <u>line</u> and <u>don't</u>.

School–Home Connection

Ask your child to read the word *water* in the box. Ask him or her to write a sentence about a person whose job might involve water, such as a farmer who waters crops.

12

Challenge
© Harcourt • Grade 1 • Book 2

▶ **Read about Sam's camping trip. Then complete the sentences.**

Sam has fun camping. He is with his mom and dad. Sam digs in the sand next to the water. He runs up a hill to see a big tree. Sam has fun. He hops on and off a log. He rests on the cot in his tent. Sam likes to camp.

_____

1. Sam has fun _____.

_____

▶ **What does Sam do? Write details about how Sam has fun.**

_____

2. _____

_____

_____

_____

_____

_____

🖊 **Try This**

Draw a picture that shows details about the things Sam did on his camping trip.

School–Home Connection

Encourage your child to write sentences that give details about a favorite toy or a place he or she likes to go.

Challenge

▶ **Write a word from the box to complete each sentence.**

skin	sled	slid	small
sniff	spend	still	swam

1. I went down a hill on my _____.

2. I _____ fast down the hill.

3. It was a _____ hill.

4. I _____ had a good time.

5. I _____ a lot of time on that hill.

 Try This

Choose a word from the box and write it in a sentence.
Draw a picture for your sentence.

 School–Home Connection

Together, think of other words that begin with
sk, sl, sm, sn, sp, st, or *sw.* Help your child write
each word. Read the list together.

14

▶ **Use the letters to make new words. Use the words to complete the sentences. Draw a picture for each sentence.**

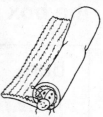

g u h m b		
b u r t g		

1. I have a _____.
   _____

2. I sat on a _____.
   _____

School–Home Connection
Write the words *snug* and *plump*. Ask your child
to read each word and then use it in a sentence.

 16

Challenge
© Harcourt • Grade 1 • Book 2

▶ **Look at each picture. Write words from the box to complete each rhyme.**

bun	cub	duck	fluff	jug	jump
rug	run	stuck	stuff	stump	tub

1. a _____ in a

_____

_____

2. a _____ on a

_____

_____

3. a _____ that

_____

_____

can _____

4. a _____

_____

_____

Challenge
© Harcourt • Grade 1 • Book 2

▶ **Write a word from the box to complete each sentence.**

be	does	food	grow	live	many

1. Ant _____ not want to get lost.

2. There are so _____ rocks. She can't see where to go at first.

3. She is hungry, so she looks for _____.

4. There must _____ a path back to her home.

5. Ant will _____ up and will help lost ants.

Try This

Use the word live to write a new sentence about Ant.
Draw a picture.

School–Home Connection

Invite your child to read all of the words in the box. Ask your child to think of a sentence that uses two or more of the words from the box.

Challenge

▶ **Read the story about the class trip.**
Then write three details about the trip.

Beth's class is at a pond. They look at many plants.
Some plants are tall and thin. Some are small. Some
have fat, pink buds at the tops of the stems. Some
plants have big, red flowers. Beth and her class have
fun looking at all the plants.

_____

- -

_____

- -

_____

- -

_____

- -

_____

 **Try This**

Write a sentence that adds another detail to the story.

 School–Home Connection

Ask your child to read the story to you. Invite
your child to add a detail that tells what he or
she would like to see at a pond.

20

Challenge
© Harcourt • Grade 1 • Book 2

Name _____

▶ **Draw lines to make words.**
   Write the words in the box.

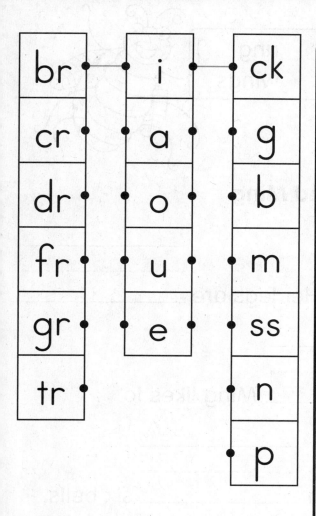

br	i	ck
cr	a	g
dr	o	b
fr	u	m
gr	e	ss
tr		n
		p

brick

School–Home Connection

Have your child read aloud the words he or
she made. Together, think of other words that
begin with *br*, *cr*, *dr*, *fr*, *gr*, and *tr*.

Challenge
© Harcourt • Grade 1 • Book 2

▶ **Write the word from the box that completes each sentence.**

bang	long	Ming	ring
song	stung	swing	wings

A Bug Called Ming

_____
_ _ _ _ _ _ _ _ _ _ _ _ _ _
_____ is a bug. Her legs are _____.

_____
_ _ _ _ _ _ _ _ _ _ _ _ _
She has two _____. Ming likes to

_____   _____
_ _ _ _ _ _ _ _ _ _ _   _ _ _ _ _ _ _ _ _ _ _
_____. She can _____ six bells.

_____
_ _ _ _ _ _ _ _ _ _ _
She can sing a _____
for you, too.

School–Home Connection

Encourage your child to think of another word
with *ng* and use it to write a sentence that tells
something else about Ming, the bug.

23

Challenge
© Harcourt • Grade 1 • Book 2

▶ **Draw lines to make words with ng.**
Write the words in the box.

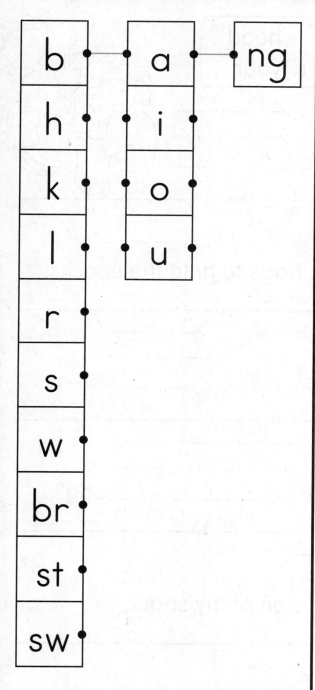

bang

Challenge
© Harcourt • Grade 1 • Book 2

▶ **Write a word from the box to complete each sentence.**

arms	every	feet	head
school	use	way	your

_____

1. Let's bring snacks to _____.

_____

2. We will _____ bags to hold the snacks.

_____

3. Jeff's snack bag fell on his _____.

_____

4. Do you have good food in _____ bag?

_____

5. I will eat _____ bit of my snack.

_____

6. Liz went that _____ with her bag.

Challenge
© Harcourt • Grade 1 • Book 2

▶ **Read the story. Then write a sentence to answer each question.**

Sam and his pals want to have fun. "Let's hop up the hill like frogs," he says.

Meg says, "I can't. See my leg?"

Sam and his pals make a plan so that Meg can have fun, too. Meg rests as they hop up and down the hill. Hop! Hop! Hop! There they go!

Meg bangs a drum as they hop. She tells them who hops best.

"This is fun!" Meg says.

1. What does Sam want to do?

_____

- -

_____

2. What does Meg tell him?

_____

- -

_____

3. At the end, how do they all have fun?

_____

- -

_____

- -

_____

School–Home Connection

Talk about a story that you and your child know. Name the important events.

Challenge
© Harcourt • Grade 1 • Book 2

▶ **Look at each picture. Write a contraction from the box to complete the sentence.**

I'll	you'll	he'll	She'll	We'll	they'll

1. "You are fast, Tom. I think _____ win."

_____

2. Beth likes milk. _____ drink it all.

_____

3. "I can do it, Mom. _____ help you."

_____

4. "Tom and I are hungry. _____ eat now."

School–Home Connection

Have your child read each completed sentence aloud. Ask him or her to say sentences using the words _he'll_ and _they'll_.

Challenge

▶ **Write the word from the box that completes each sentence.**

corn	forget	store	for	Doris	more

The Pet Store

Greg went to the pet _____. It has food

_____ _____

_____ his fish. He got _____

food there. Greg fed _____ to a rabbit.

Then he and _____ went to pet a kitten.

Greg will not _____ his trip to the pet store.

School–Home Connection

Have your child read the story to you. Ask him or her to think of other words with the *or* sound. Help him or her write the words.

30

Challenge
© Harcourt • Grade 1 • Book 2

▶ **Read each sentence. Circle the word in each sentence that has the same vowel sound as <u>for</u>. Write the word on the line.**

1. This kitten is for Don. _____

_____

2. A fox snored as it slept. _____

_____

3. I got up this morning. _____

_____

4. The lamp cord is long. _____

_____

5. He dropped his fork. _____

_____

6. I want one more muffin. _____

_____

7. Mom forgot the food. _____

School–Home Connection

Write the words *fog, for,* and *form.* Talk about how the words are alike and different. Repeat this activity with *stop, storm,* and *store.*

32

▶ **Write a word from the box to complete each sentence.**

| animals | cold | fish | from |
| their | under | very | |

_____
- -

1. Mr. Morris has six _____.

_____
- -

2. His rabbit hid _____ my desk.

_____
- -

3. The duck eats _____ my hand.

_____
- -

4. The two kittens are _____ soft.

_____
- -

5. All the animals like _____ home.

Try This

Write a sentence about your favorite animal, using a word from the box.

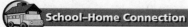
School–Home Connection
Have your child write about fish, using all the words from the box.

33

Name _____

▶ **Look at the two buildings.**

 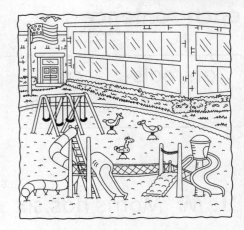

▶ **Write one sentence telling how they are the same.**
Write one sentence telling how they are different.

_____

1. _____

_____

_____

2. _____

_____

 **Try This**

Think of another building you have seen. Write a sentence
telling how it is different from the buildings above.

School–Home Connection

Ask your child to think of two animals.
Together, talk about how they are alike and
how they are different.

 34

▶ **Use a word from each box to make a compound word that names the picture. Use the word in a sentence. Draw a line under the compound word.**

ant	back	bath		box	corn	hill
pop	sand	sun		pack	set	tub

1. _____
   - - - - - - - - - - - - - - - -
   _____

   _____

2. _____
   - - - - - - - - - - - - - - - -
   _____

   _____

3. _____
   - - - - - - - - - - - - - - - -
   _____

School–Home Connection

Talk about the meaning of each word your
child used in a sentence. Ask your child to use
each compound word in a new sentence.

35

Challenge
© Harcourt • Grade 1 • Book 2

► **Write a word from the box to complete each sentence.**

| catfish | vanish | finished | fishing |
| shortcut | wish | hush | |

The Fishing Trip

_____

I am going _____ with my dad.

_____

We take the _____ to the pond.

_____

There are _____ in the pond.

_____

I must _____, or the fish will

_____

_____. Now we are going home.

_____

The fishing trip is _____.

 **School–Home Connection**

Have your child read the completed story aloud. Ask him or her to use the word *wish* to write another sentence for the story.

▶ **Write a word from the box to complete each sentence.**

cash	finished	shop	relish
shelf	rush	shock	wished

_____
- -

1. We will _____ for Mom's gift.

_____
- -

2. Dad has _____ to get it.

_____
- -

3. There's a red hat on the _____.

_____
- -

4. My mom _____ for a hat.

_____
- -

5. We are _____.

🖊 **Try This**

Choose a word from the box. Write a sentence of your own.

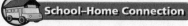
School–Home Connection

Have your child read each completed sentence aloud. Together, think of other words that have *sh* in them.

Challenge

▶ **Write the word that completes the sentence.**

came	Could	gold	happy
made	night	saw	were

_____

1. Tess _____ a puppet out of a worn sock.

_____

2. There _____ two arms and two legs on it.

"_____

3. _____ I use a doll dress?" Tess asked Ann.

_____

4. Tess added a _____ wig to her puppet.

_____

5. Kim and Josh _____ to see the sock puppet.

🖊 **Try This**

Use <u>night</u>, <u>saw</u>, or <u>happy</u> in a sentence about the puppet.

🚌 **School–Home Connection**

Have your child read each completed sentence aloud. Have him or her read each word in the box and use it in a sentence.

40

▶ **Read each story. Then write what the setting is.**

One morning, Frank went to the store. He wanted new pots and pans.

"I want to see your best pots and pans," Frank said.

"We have no pots. We have no pans," the man said. "This store is for sporting goods. We sell bats, balls, and tennis rackets."

1. _____

"Come on, Rick!" Beth yelled. "Let's hop from rock to rock to the pond."

"No," said Rick. "I want to look for frogs in the grass."

"There are frogs in the water," Beth said.

"Good! Let's look!" said Rick. "Then we have to go home to eat dinner."

2. _____

School–Home Connection
Ask your child to describe another setting. Talk about things you could do in this setting.

41

Challenge
© Harcourt • Grade 1 • Book 2

Name _____

▶ **Write the words where they belong in the puzzle.**

slept	grab	skunk
blanket	trumpet	clock

1. This can go on a bed.

2. You do this with your hands.

3. This animal can smell bad.

4. This tells the time.

5. You can play this in a band.

6. You did this last night.

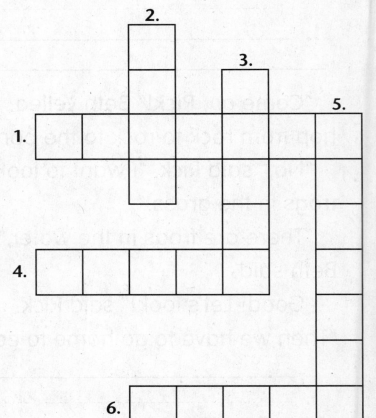

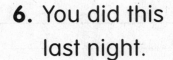

School–Home Connection

Take turns thinking of words that begin with *dr*, *fl*, *sn*, or *st*. Say a clue, and then let the other person guess the word.

Challenge

© Harcourt • Grade 1 • Book 2

Reach for the Stars

Book 1-3

▶ **Write the word from the box that completes each sentence.**

> chest   champs   pitch   bunch
> catch   stretch   children

_____

1. A _____ of us play ball.

_____

_____

2. More _____ watch us.

_____

_____

3. Janet can _____ the ball.

_____

_____

4. I _____ a fastball to Chuck.

_____

_____

5. We win! We are the _____.

School–Home Connection

Have your child read the sentences aloud.
Encourage your child to use the unused words
in the box to write more sentences.

2

Challenge

▶ **Circle the sentence that tells about the picture.**

1. Mitch is in the ketchup.

Mitch is in the kitchen.

Mitch is in the chest.

2. He will munch on a branch.

He has such an itch.

He has a sandwich for lunch.

3. There's not much punch left.

He will stitch the patch.

The children eat chips.

4. Mitch will fetch the crutch.

Mitch chats with Chuck.

Mitch checks for milk.

 School–Home Connection

Have your child read each sentence aloud.
Point to one set of sentences, and ask him or
her to underline all the words with the sound
of *ch*, as in *chin*.

4

Name _____

▶ **Write a word from the box to complete each sentence.**

| air | fly | friends | grew |
| need | play | rain | watch |

_____

----

1. I like to _____ my kitten.

_____

_____

----

2. My kitten jumps into the _____.

_____

_____

----

3. My dog got wet in the _____.

_____

_____

----

4. He _____ up to be a big dog!

✎ **Try This**

Write a new sentence with one of the words you did not use. Draw a picture to go with it.

🚌 **School–Home Connection**

Have your child read each sentence. Encourage your child to use words from the box to write other sentences about animals.

Challenge
© Harcourt • Grade 1 • Book 3

Name _____

▶ **Write 1, 2, or 3 to put the pictures in order. Then write a sentence to tell what happens in each picture.**

1. First, _____

2. Next, _____

3. Last, _____

School–Home Connection

Have your child tell you what is happening in the pictures in the correct order. Ask: *What do you think will happen next?*

6

Challenge
© Harcourt • Grade 1 • Book 3

▶ **Write a word from the box to complete each sentence. Add _es_ if it is needed.**

| catch   mix   glass   radish |

In the Kitchen

_____

Chad _____ the eggs.

Mom chops some _____.

Mom drops a _____.

Chad _____ it.

Chad gets out two _____.

He drops one _____.

Will Mom _____ it?

School–Home Connection

Have your child read the story aloud to you.
Then write the word *buzz*, and have your child
read it aloud. Ask him or her to write the word
buzzes.

7

Challenge

Name _____

▶ **Write a word from the box to complete each sentence.**

yarn	card	mark	dart
farm	backyard	star	charming

1. I'll make a _____ for Mom.

2. It will have a big _____ on it.

3. I must find the red _____.

4. I will _____ where the pumpkins go.

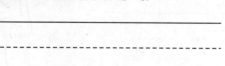

5. Mom will think it's a

_____

_____ card.

Challenge
© Harcourt • Grade 1 • Book 3

▶ **Write a word from the box to complete each sentence.**

arm	darling	car	dark
barnyard	started	farm	far

At the Farm

_____

We went in the _____

to visit a _____. We didn't have

_____   _____

_____ to go. I saw a _____

little pig in the _____.

It had a _____ spot on its head.

I _____ to pet it, and then

it sniffed my _____.

School–Home Connection

Have your child read the story to you. Ask him
or her to think of a word with *ar* and to write
an additional sentence for the story.

11

▶ **Write words from the box to complete each sentence.**

again	feel	house	know
loud	Mrs.	put	say

_____

1. Mr. and _____ Martin are at my

_____

_____ .

_____

2. I _____ happy as I _____

good morning.

_____

3. I _____ out my hand and say good

morning _____ .

 **Try This**

Write a new sentence with two words from the box.
Draw a picture.

School–Home Connection

Have your child read each completed sentence
aloud. Then ask him or her to use words from
the box to write about things that are *loud*
and things people *know*.

12

Challenge

▶ **Write a sentence that tells why the author might have written each story.**

Helping Lost Pets by Liz Smith

I have a dog called Max. Max has a tag. The tag tells where his home is. It tells who to call if Max is lost. If you find a lost pet, look at its tag. The tag can tell you who to call.

1. _____
_____
_____

Dog Fun! by Martin Hill

Bark! Sniff! Run and jump. Lick! Wag! Thump, thump, thump! Let's go to the park! Let's have fun! I'll catch the ball. I'll run and run!

2. _____
_____
_____

School–Home Connection

With your child, think of an animal story that is meant to entertain readers. Then talk about what an author might say to teach people about animals.

13

► **Add s, ed, or ing to each word.**
Write the new word in the sentence.

1. I helped Dad as he was _____ the porch.

   dust

2. We _____ the flower pots.

   stack

3. Dad sings as he _____ up sticks.

   pick

4. I _____ my leg on the bench.

   bump

5. Dad and I were _____ the bench.

   lift

School–Home Connection

Have your child read each completed sentence aloud. Ask your child to tell why he or she chose each word ending.

14

Challenge
© Harcourt • Grade 1 • Book 3

▶ **Read the sentences. Circle the sentence that tells about the picture.**

1.

   Cliff has a quilt on his bed.

   Cliff has a quack on his bed.

   Cliff has a quick on his bed.

2.

   I think I like to swim.

   I will quit eating corn.

   When will my eggs hatch?

3.

   The ball is on a quilt.

   Which ball do you want?

   That ball is in the pond.

4.

   Ducks thick all day.

   Ducks quick all day.

   Ducks quack all day.

5.

   He quits the ball.

   He thinks the ball is black.

   He whacks the ball hard.

School–Home Connection

Have your child point to the words *quack* and *whacks*. Talk about how the words are alike and how they are different.

16

▶ **Write the word from the box to complete the sentence.**

| Which | thing | quick | quit | When | Quinn |

1. Do you think he is _____ ?

2. _____ holds a shell in his hand.

3. _____ can I go out to play?

4. _____ one is my gift?

✐ **Try This**

Write a sentence. Use two words from the box.

School–Home Connection

Have your child read each sentence aloud.
Together, think of other words that begin with
qu and *wh*.

18

▶ **Write a word from the box to complete each sentence.**

about	books	people	family
name	read	work	writing

_____

----

1. There are many _____ in my school.

_____

_____

----

2. I like to _____ every morning.

_____

_____

----

3. My _____ is very happy to visit my class.

_____

_____

----

4. Martin is _____ with his black marker.

_____

_____

----

5. He will rush to finish his _____ .

Try This

Write a new sentence. Use two words from the box.

19

Challenge

Name _____

▶ **Look at the pictures. Write 1, 2, or 3 to
tell the order of the events. Then write
a sentence to tell about each event. Use
the words first, next, and last.**

1. _____

_____

2. _____

_____

3. _____

_____

School–Home Connection

Let your child tell you the correct order of
events shown in the pictures. Ask: *Could these
events take place in a different order?*

20

Challenge
© Harcourt • Grade 1 • Book 3

Name _____

▶ **Add ed or ing to each word. Write the word in the sentence.**

pop

_____

- -

1. Marvin _____ popcorn.

_____

mop

_____

- -

2. Kim is _____ the porch.

_____

flap

_____

- -

3. The hen _____ its wings.

_____

stop

_____

- -

4. It _____ raining this morning.

_____

slip

_____

- -

5. They were _____ in the mud.

School–Home Connection

Write the words *clap* and *skip*. Have your child
rewrite each word, adding *-ed* and *-ing*. Ask
him or her to say sentences with the words.

21

Challenge
© Harcourt • Grade 1 • Book 3

Name _____

▶ **Read the clues. Then write the words where they belong in the puzzle.**

herd	sir	fur
squirrel	purr	verse

1. This animal likes nuts. **2.** A man is called this.

3. A cat can do this. **4.** Dogs have this.

5. This is part of a song. **6.** Many animals are in this.

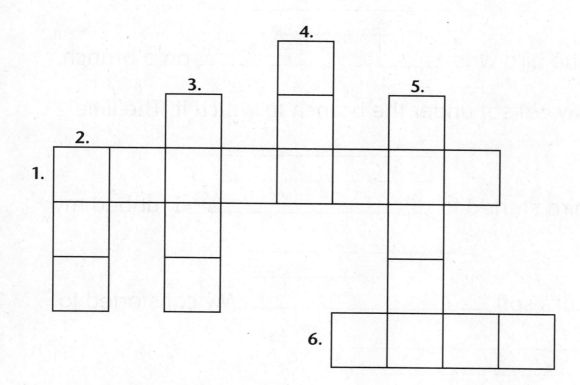

School–Home Connection
Write the words *third*, *thunder*, *dirt*, and *hurt*.
Together, arrange the words to make your own
crossword puzzle.

23

Challenge
© Harcourt • Grade 1 • Book 3

Name _____

▶ **Write a word from the box to complete each sentence.**

purr	bird	dirt
chirp	perched	fur

A Bird in My Yard

My cat saw a _____ in the backyard.

The bird was _____ on a branch.

My cat sat under the branch to watch it. The little

bird started to _____. I rubbed my

cat's soft _____. My cat started to

_____. It forgot about the little bird.

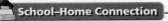
25

Challenge

▶ **Write the word that completes the sentence.**

| always | join | Cow's | by |
| please | nice | room | |

_____

1. _____ home is in a barn.

_____

2. It is a very _____ barn to live in.

_____

3. It has a lot of _____ for animals.

_____

4. Cow _____ likes to have friends over.

" _____

5. _____, come back soon," she tells them.

▶ **Read the story. Answer the questions.**

Hen's New Dress

Hen's new dress didn't fit. It hung down past her feet. It hid her arms and legs. Duck said she could hem it. Then Hen said, "I could eat more. Then I'll grow into it!"

1. What hung down past Hen's feet?

_____

- -

_____

2. What did Duck say she could do?

_____

- -

_____

3. What is "Hen's New Dress" about?

_____

- -

_____

_____

- -

_____

_____

- -

School–Home Connection

Have your child think of a story he or she knows. Ask him or her to draw a picture that shows what the story is mainly about.

27

Challenge
© Harcourt • Grade 1 • Book 3

Name _____

▶ **Use a word from the box to complete each sentence. You will need to add er or est to some of the words.**

fresh	long	fast	tall	loud

_____

1. The cactus is _____ than the fern.

_____

2. This muffin is _____ .

_____

3. Dennis is the _____ singer.

_____

4. I had a _____ nap than Dad.

_____

5. That girl is the _____ .

School–Home Connection

Have your child draw pictures to compare three things. Ask him or her to label each picture with a word, adding *-er* or *-est* where it is needed. For example, *tall, taller, tallest.*

28

Challenge
© Harcourt • Grade 1 • Book 3

▶ **Write a word from the box to match the clue.**

turtle	rattle	pickle
pebble	saddle	shuffle

_____

1. This can go on a sandwich. _____

_____

2. This is a small rock. _____

_____

3. You do this to a deck of cards. _____

_____

4. You put this on a horse. _____

_____

5. This animal has a shell. _____

Try This

Write the words <u>tickle</u> and <u>giggle</u> in a sentence.

School–Home Connection

Together, think of other words that end with *-le*. Make up clues for each word.

30

Challenge
© Harcourt • Grade 1 • Book 3

▶ **Write a word from the box to complete the sentence.**

wobbles	cuddle	purple	little
middle	uncle	startle	sparkles

Nell's New Doll

_____

Nell got a _____ doll. It was

_____

from her _____. The doll has

_____

a _____ dress. The dress has

_____

_____ on it. Nell likes to

_____

_____ her new doll. She puts it

_____

in the _____ of her bed.

School–Home Connection

Have your child read the completed story
aloud. Point to the words *wobbles* and *startle*.
Encourage your child to write one of the words
in a sentence.

32

Challenge
© Harcourt • Grade 1 • Book 3

▶ **Write the word that completes the sentence.**

buy	carry	money	other
paint	paper	would	

DOG TOYS

1. Jeff will _____ food for his dog.

2. He has _____ in his pocket.

3. Jeff gets _____ things, too.

4. The man puts it all in a _____ bag.

5. Jeff will _____ the bag home.

Try This

Write a sentence with a word you did not use.

School–Home Connection

Write each word on a slip of paper or a card. Turn the words face down. Take turns choosing a word and using it in a sentence.

Challenge

Name _____

▶ **Read the paragraph. Write the main idea. Then write the details.**

Many animals live in ponds. You can find fish in ponds. Frogs hatch from eggs in ponds. Some otters live in ponds, too.

Main Idea

Details

Ask your child to read the paragraph aloud. Together, think of a title for the paragraph.

Challenge
© Harcourt • Grade 1 • Book 3

Name _____

▶ **Add ed or ing to the word to complete
the sentence. Remember to double the
final consonant.**

pet

_____

- -

1. She is _____ the dog.

_____

jog

_____

- -

2. My sister _____ with me.

_____

pop

_____

- -

3. The popcorn is _____ now.

_____

stop

_____

- -

4. Chad _____ playing to eat lunch.

_____

plan

_____

- -

5. Helen is _____ to get a cat.

🚌 **School–Home Connection**

Write the words *hop* and *pack*. **Ask your child**
which word needs the last letter doubled when
ed or *ing* is added. *(hop)*

35

Challenge
© Harcourt • Grade 1 • Book 3

▶ **Read the clues. Then write the words
where they belong in the puzzle.**

| crow | elbow | pillow | rowboat |
| soap | toad | toast | window |

1. This will get you across a pond.

2. This is a black bird.

3. This helps you see in or out.

4. This looks like a frog.

5. This is good with jam.

6. This is part of your arm.

7. You use this in a bath.

8. You put your head on it.

Challenge
© Harcourt • Grade 1 • Book 3

▶ **Write a word from the box to complete the sentence.**

blowing	throw	row	moaned
coat	snow	loaned	window

The Big Snowstorm

_____

The _____ fell for six days in a

_____ _____. I sat at the _____

_____

and _____. Then the wind stopped

_____ _____

_____. "Let's go _____

_____

snowballs!" Joan said. I put on my _____,

_____

and she _____ me a hat.

Challenge
© Harcourt • Grade 1 • Book 3

Name _____

▶ **Write the word that completes
the sentence.**

mouse	our	over
pretty	surprise	three

1. Robin has a _____ little dog.

2. She went _____ to Clark's house.

3. Clark had a _____ for Robin.

4. Her dog will have _____ new
friends.

Try This

Write sentences with the words <u>our</u> and <u>mouse</u>.

School–Home Connection

Ask your child to read the completed
sentences. Point to the word *surprise,* and talk
about different ways to use the word.

40

▶ **Read the story. Then tell why you think the author wrote this story.**

Winter Fun
by Fred West

   A cold winter day can be fun. All you need is snow! First, make three big snowballs. Pack them hard. Then stack them up. Start with the biggest. Put one in the middle. Put the smallest on top.

   Find two good sticks. Use them to make arms. Find some pebbles. Use them to make two eyes, a happy grin, and more. Put a hat on top. Now you have made a snow surprise!

_____

- -

_____

- -

_____

_____

- -

_____

Try This

Write a sentence. Tell how you think the author feels about snow.

School–Home Connection

Talk about what your child might want to
teach someone how to do.

41

Challenge

▶ **Write a word from the box to complete the sentence.**

coast	flown	grown	own
roasted	shown	thrown	toast

Uncle Ted's Visit

_____

I made _____ and jam for Uncle

_____

Ted. "Ellen, you have _____ up

_____

so fast," he said. "Has your mom _____

you how to play softball?" I said, "Yes, I have my

_____

_____ mitt!" Uncle Ted and I played catch

_____

in the yard. After we had _____ the ball

_____

all morning, we rested. Then we _____

hot dogs for lunch.

School–Home Connection

Have your child read the completed story aloud. Talk about the meanings of *coast* and *flown*. Ask your child to use the words to write more sentences for the story.

42

Challenge
© Harcourt • Grade 1 • Book 3

Make Your Mark

Book 1-4

▶ **Read each sentence. Circle the word that has the same vowel sound as <u>beach</u>. Write the word.**

_____

- -

1. Look at this beautiful peach. _____

_____

_____

- - - - - - - - - - - - - - - - - - - -

2. Doreen talks with her mother. _____

_____

_____

- -

3. He ran faster than Bill. _____

_____

_____

- - - - - - - - - - - - - - - - - - - -

4. The eagle likes fish. _____

_____

_____

- -

5. Jim follows Herbert to each job. _____

_____

_____

- - - - - - - - - - - - - - - - - - - -

6. Ask Tom to clean his room. _____

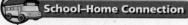

School–Home Connection

Ask your child to read aloud one of the
sentences. Together, think of words that
rhyme with the circled word.

Challenge

Name _____

▶ **Draw lines to make words with the
long e sound. Write the words in the box.
One has been done for you.**

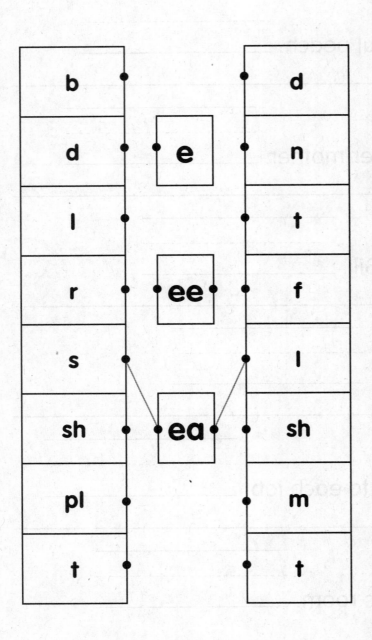

seal

School–Home Connection
Have your child read aloud the words he or she
completed.

Challenge
© Harcourt • Grade 1 • Book 4

▶ **Use the words in the box to write a story about the picture.**

┌───┐
│ door   hurry   mother   dear   should   sky   told │
└───┘

_____

- -

_____

- -

_____

- -

_____

- -

_____

- -

_____

- -

School–Home Connection

Have your child read the completed story aloud.
Then ask your child to think of a sentence
using more than one word from the box.

5

Challenge

▶ **Look at the picture. Write a sentence
that tells why it happened.**

What Happened?	Why Did It Happen?
1.  The vase broke.	_____
2.  They got wet.	_____
3.  She put on a jacket.	_____

School–Home Connection

Ask your child to tell something that happened
today and why it happened.

6

Challenge

© Harcourt • Grade 1 • Book 4

▶ **Add 've or 're. Write the new word in the sentence.**

1. _____ added two plus three.
   You

2. _____ going to play at my house.
   We

3. _____ gone to the library.
   They

4. _____ very good at reading.
   You

5. _____ brushed my teeth.
   I

School–Home Connection

Have your child use each answer in a sentence
of his or her own.

7

Name _____

▶ **Look at each picture. Circle the sentence that tells about it. Then write a sentence to go with the last picture.**

1.

Carl and Robert wait for the bus.

The paint is at the bus stop.

_____

2.

Jane plays with the popcorn.

Jane pays for the popcorn.

_____

3.

He plays in the rain.

He may not go out in the rain.

_____

4.

The pig stays away from the bucket.

The pig eats grain from a bucket.

_____

5.

_ _ _ _ _ _ _ _ _ _ _ _ _ _ _ _ _ _ _ _

_____

_ _ _ _ _ _ _ _ _ _ _ _ _ _ _ _ _ _ _ _

_____

School–Home Connection

Have your child read each sentence aloud. Ask him or her to point to the words that have the long a vowel sound.

9

Challenge
© Harcourt • Grade 1 • Book 4

▶ **Read each sentence. Circle the word that has the long a sound, as in hay. Write the word on the line.**

_____

1. Carl used bait to catch fish. _____

_____

2. "May I pet the cat?" _____

_____

3. "Hooray, our team wins!" _____

_____

4. Kirk paid for the apple at the market. _____

_____

5. Arthur turned six on Sunday. _____

_____

6. Do not run in the hallway. _____

 **School–Home Connection**

Ask your child to read the sentences aloud.
Together, think of words that rhyme with some
of the words he or she circled.

11

Challenge
© Harcourt • Grade 1 • Book 4

▶ **Use the words in the box to write a story about the picture.**

cool	dry	four	holes
move	place	warm	

_____

- -

_____

- -

_____

- -

_____

- -

_____

- -

_____

- -

_____

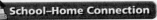

School–Home Connection

Ask your child to read each word in the box and
use the word in a sentence. Together, look at
the picture and talk about what is happening.

12

Challenge
© Harcourt • Grade 1 • Book 4

Name _____

▶ **A. Look at the picture. Write what happened and why it happened.**

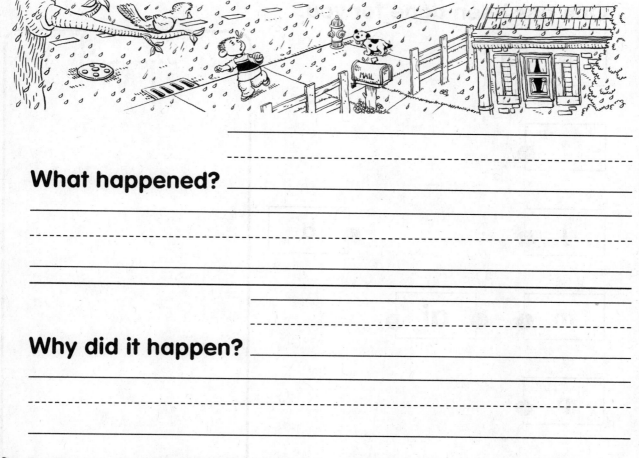

What happened? _____

_____

_____

Why did it happen? _____

_____

_____

▶ **B. Draw a picture. On the back of this paper, write what happened and why it happened.**

 **School–Home Connection**

Have your child explain what happens in each
picture and why. Together, make up a story to
go with one of the pictures.

13

Challenge
© Harcourt • Grade 1 • Book 4

Name _____

▶ **Draw lines to make words with the long a sound. Write the words in the box. One has been done for you.**

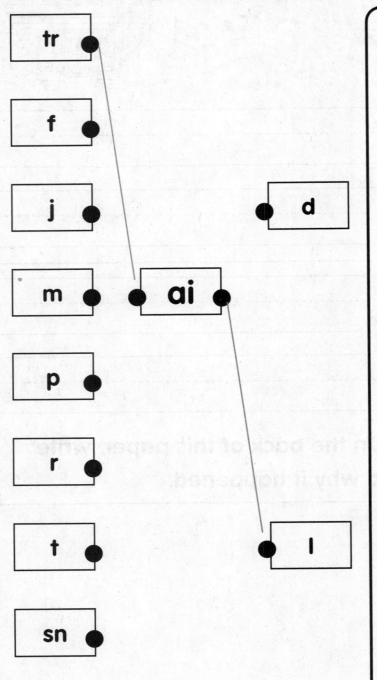

trail

Challenge
© Harcourt • Grade 1 • Book 4

▶ **Circle the sentence that tells about each picture.**

1. Mom's friend Kate was late.
The food was at the lake.

_____

2. Mom gave a grape to the ape.
Mom made me wait to eat.

_____

3. Kate had a vase.
Kate came at last.

_____

4. I paste a shape on the plate.
I ate all the food on my plate.

_____

5. Then it was time for the cake.
The cake was in the shape of a snake.

_____

6. The cake was not baked.
After we ate cake, we played a game.

16

Challenge
© Harcourt • Grade 1 • Book 4

▶ **Write a word from the box to complete each sentence.**

ate	base	Kate	chase
waste	baseball	game	stale

The Game

_____
- -
_____ and Beth were sitting on a

_____
- -

bench. They were at a _____. Dad

_____
- -

played _____. He hit the ball. Then he

_____
- - - - - - - - - - - - - - - - - - - -

ran to first _____. The other team had

_____
- - - - - - - - - - - - - - - - - - -

to _____ the ball. Dad's team won!

_____
- -

The two teams _____ lunch together.

Challenge
© Harcourt • Grade 1 • Book 4

▶ **Use the words in the box to write a story about the picture.**

around	found	near	tired
might	open	gone	hears

_____
- - - - - - - - - - - - - - - -
_____
- - - - - - - - - - - - - - - -
_____
- - - - - - - - - - - - - - - -
_____
- - - - - - - - - - - - - - - -
_____
- - - - - - - - - - - - - - - -
_____
- - - - - - - - - - - - - - - -
_____
- - - - - - - - - - - - - - - -
_____

 **School–Home Connection**

Ask your child to read his or her story to you.
Talk about other things he or she might see
around a lake.

19

Name _____

▶ **Think about the problem in each
picture. Write a sentence that tells
a way to solve the problem.**

1. _____

_____

_____

2. _____

_____

_____

3. _____

_____

_____

Try This

Draw a picture that shows a problem. Then draw a
picture that shows how to solve the problem.

School–Home Connection

With your child, look around your home for
possible problems. Have your child think of
ways to solve any problems you find.

20

Challenge

Name _____

▶ **Write a word from the box to
complete each sentence.**

lane	grade	crane	Jane
plane	made	trade	Shane

The Trade

_____

I met a girl on the _____. Her name is

_____

_____. She gave me a frog puppet. "I

_____

_____ it in class," she said. "My teacher gave

_____

me a good _____ for it." I gave Jane

my seashell. "I will share this with my little brother

_____

_____," she said. We agreed that it was a

_____

good _____.

21

Challenge
© Harcourt • Grade 1 • Book 4

Name _____

▶ **Complete each sentence with a word
that has the long i sound as in <u>kite</u>.**

_____

- - - - - - - - - - - - - - - - -

1. Chuck _____ the apple.

_____

_____

- - - - - - - - - - - - - - -

2. It is _____ to go home now.

_____

_____

- - - - - - - - - - - - - -

3. He _____ when he is happy.

_____

_____

- - - - - - - - - - - - - - -

4. Mom will _____ Glen to school.

_____

_____

- - - - - - - - - - - - - - -

5. We _____ to school on a bus.

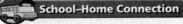 **Try This**

Write a sentence that uses the words <u>slid</u> and <u>slide</u>.

School–Home Connection

Have your child make up more sentences using
the words that he or she wrote.

 23

Challenge
© Harcourt • Grade 1 • Book 4

▶ **Read each sentence. Unscramble the letters to make a word to complete each sentence.**

ievh   1. The bees stay in the _____.

kehis   2. Fred _____ up the hill.

imche   3. The bells will _____.

ienn   4. Her sister is _____ years old.

htwie   5. She has a _____ shirt.

pnie   6. They sit under the _____ tree.

tkei   7. We pick the best _____ to buy.

School–Home Connection
Say the words *hid, hide, rip, ripe, slim,* and *slime.* Ask your child to write the words as you say them.

Challenge
© Harcourt • Grade 1 • Book 4

▶ **Use the words in the box to write a
story about the picture.**

| because | light | right | those | walked |

_____

- -

_____

- -

_____

- -

_____

- -

_____

- -

_____

Challenge
© Harcourt • Grade 1 • Book 4

Name _____

▶ **Each picture shows a problem. Write a sentence that tells what one solution might be.**

I.

_____

- -

_____

- -

_____

2.

_____

- -

_____

- -

_____

3.

_____

- -

_____

- -

_____

✎ **Try This**

Write a sentence that tells another solution to one of the problems.

🚌 **School–Home Connection**

Point to each picture. Have your child explain the problem it shows. Talk about other possible solutions.

27

▶ **Read each sentence. Choose a word from the box. Add -ed or -ing to make a word that will complete each sentence.**

hide	smile	drive	surprise	bake

_____
- -

1. Mom _____ a cake.

_____

_____
- -

2. She is _____ it from Dad.

_____

_____
- -

3. We are _____ him for his birthday.

_____

_____
- -

4. He will be _____ home.

_____

_____
- -

5. Soon Dad will be _____.

School–Home Connection

Write the words *hike*, *shake*, and *save*. Have
your child write new words by adding *-ed*
and *-ing* to each.

28

▶ **Write a word from the box to complete each sentence.**

drove	rode	dozed	hose
tadpole	chose	molehill	note

1. Dad _____ on the deck.

2. I _____ Gail for my team.

3. James put a _____ in the mail.

4. The children _____ on a bus.

5. My teacher _____ a van.

30

Challenge

© Harcourt • Grade 1 • Book 4

▶ **Write a word from the box to complete each sentence.**

roses	jokes	Cole	rope
hose	home	nose	doze

The Garden

_____   _____

_____ is at _____

with his mom and dad. They work in the yard on

a hot day. Cole waters the garden with the

_____

_____. Cole's dad plants

_____

_____. Cole smells them with

_____

his _____. His mother tells

_____

_____ while they work.

Challenge

© Harcourt • Grade 1 • Book 4

Name _____

► **Use the words in the box to write a story about the picture.**

brown	hello	loudly
love	pulled	city

_____

- -

_____

- -

_____

- -

_____

- -

_____

- -

_____

School–Home Connection

Have your child read the story to you. Talk about other things your child might see on a city street. Encourage him or her to use the words in the box as you talk.

33

Challenge
© Harcourt • Grade 1 • Book 4

Name _____

▶ **Read the story. Then draw a conclusion
about the boys. Write it in a sentence.**

Seth and Mark go up high on the swings at the
park. Then they skip to the slide. The boys take turns
sliding down.

At Mark's house, they eat popcorn on the porch. Then
the boys take out their math books. Seth helps Mark do
his math work. Then it's time for Seth to go home. "I'll
see you at school!" they both say at the same time.

_____
- -
_____
- -
_____
- -
_____

School–Home Connection

Ask your child what clues led to his or her
conclusion about the characters.

34

▶ **Write words from the box to complete each sentence.**

bone	pole	hole	mole
pole	shone	stone	stone

1. The _____ is in the _____ _____.

2. The sun _____ on the _____ _____.

3. The flag _____ is _____ set in _____.

School–Home Connection

Have your child read aloud the completed
sentences. Together, think of other sentences
for the words in the box.

35

Challenge
© Harcourt • Grade 1 • Book 4

▶ **Read the clues. Then write the words where they belong in the puzzle.**

age	bridge	circle
face	large	rice

1. This can help you cross over.

2. This is food.

3. This has a nose.

4. This is round.

5. This tells how old you are.

6. This means <u>big</u>.

School–Home Connection

Have your child write the words in the box on a separate sheet of paper. Then have him or her read the clues for you to guess the correct words.

Challenge
© Harcourt • Grade 1 • Book 4

▶ **Write a word from the box to complete each sentence.**

budge	center	face	force	gentle
magic	place	pranced	stage	

Brave Badger

Hedgehog and Badger had parts in a play. Hedgehog

_____   _____

_____ onto the _____,

_____

but Badger didn't _____.

_____

A _____ nudge from Rabbit didn't help.

_____

"I can't _____ you," Rabbit said, "but your

_____

_____ tricks are the best!" Then Badger

stepped onto the stage.

School–Home Connection

Have your child read the completed story aloud. Ask him or her to use the words *center*, *face*, and *place* to write more sentences for the story.

39

Challenge
© Harcourt • Grade 1 • Book 4

▶ **Use the words in the box to write a story about the picture.**

eyes	listen	visitor	remembered
become	talk	busy	high

_____

_____

_____

_____

_____

_____

 **School–Home Connection**

Have your child read the story aloud to you.
Talk about other ways to use the words in
the box.

Challenge

© Harcourt • Grade 1 • Book 4

Name _____

▶ **Read the story. Then complete the sentence.**

1.

Nick hung up a note at the store. It said Please call if you see my cat. "I hope my cat is safe," Nick said sadly. "I miss him so much."

_____

- -

Nick's cat is _____.

2.

"Get up, Jeff," Mom said. "Why are you still in bed?"

Jeff cried, "Oh Mom, my throat hurts, and my nose is stuffed up. I can't go to school today!"

_____

- -

Jeff is _____.

3.

Kate feeds her hamster, Hedge, and gives him fresh water. When Hedge is asleep, she reads about cats and dogs.

_____

- -

Kate likes _____.

Challenge
© Harcourt • Grade 1 • Book 4

Name _____

▶ **Use a word from each side of the box
to form a contraction that completes the
sentence.**

Janet	has	will
does	she	not
friend		is

_____

----

1. Janet _____ picked up her room.

_____

----

2. _____ have to clean it up soon.

_____

----

3. She _____ want to, but she should.

_____

----

4. Her _____ coming over soon.

_____

----

5. _____ picking up her room now.

School–Home Connection

Have your child read each completed sentence
aloud. Ask him or her to tell you what two
words make up each contraction.

42

Watch This!

Book 1-5

Name _____

▶ **Look at each picture. Write a word from the box to complete the sentence.**

confused	cute	excuse	flute
huge	include	mule	use

1. Janet plays a _____ as Patrick plays the drums.

2. "I must do my homework now. Please _____ _____ me."

3. She is _____ about which path to take.

4. The _____ eats oats from a bucket.

School–Home Connection

Write the words *huge* and *hug*. Talk about how the words are alike and different. Then ask your child to write the words *cub* and *cube*.

2

Challenge
© Harcourt • Grade 1 • Book 5

▶ **Write a word from the box to complete the sentence.**

used	costumes	Luke
rude	tune	flute

The Concert

I went to a concert. Luke was playing the

_____

_____. Ginger was playing

the trumpet. I liked the

_____

_____ they played. They all

_____

wore nice _____. They all

_____

_____ their music. After the show I told

_____

Ginger and _____ that they did very well.

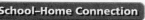
School–Home Connection

Have your child read the story aloud. Encourage
your child to write another sentence for the
story, using the word *cute* or *excuse*.

Challenge
© Harcourt • Grade 1 • Book 5

▶ **Use the words in the box to write a story about the picture.**

clear	color	good-bye	hair
	kinds	toes	only

_____

_____

_____

_____

_____

_____

_____

_____

_____

_____

_____

_____

_____

_____

 **School–Home Connection**

Ask your child to read his or her story aloud.
Have your child think of a title for the story,
using a word from the box.

 5

Challenge
© Harcourt • Grade 1 • Book 5

▶ **Each group of words is in ABC order. Add a new word on each line. Keep the words in ABC order.**

1. about	2. bird	3. _____
4. _____	5. eel	6. _____

1. kick	2. _____	3. paper
4. _____	5. thank	6. _____

1. loud	2. _____	3. _____
4. those	5. water	6. _____

School–Home Connection

Have your child read each list aloud. Then ask how he or she decided what words to add to the list.

6

Challenge
© Harcourt • Grade 1 • Book 5

Phonics: Inflections
-ed, -ing (drop e);
Inflections -ed,
-ing (double final
consonant)

Lesson 25

Name _____

▶ **Add ed or ng to the word. Choose the word that completes each sentence. Write the word in the sentence.**

| rake | clap | hope | take | make | chase |

_____

1. The cat _____ the string.

_____

2. We _____ because the play was good.

_____

3. The girls are _____ to go to the circus.

_____

4. The children are _____ turns.

_____

5. Lester is _____ popcorn for all of us.

School–Home Connection

On a separate sheet of paper, have your child write each word from the box, adding both *ing* and *ed*. Ask how each word changed.

7

Challenge
© Harcourt • Grade 1 • Book 5

▶ **Read the story. Circle all the words that have the long i sound, as in pie. Write each word where it belongs in the chart.**

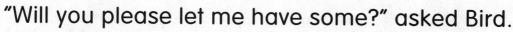

Bear baked a pie. Bird flew down and tried to eat it. He wasn't shy about eating Bear's food.

"That's my pie!" cried Bear. "You may not eat it without asking first."

"Will you please let me have some?" asked Bird. "A small bird such as myself needs to eat, too."

"All right," Bear said. "You might want to use a plate."

ie	y	igh

School–Home Connection
Write the words *fly*, *tied*, and *tight*. Encourage your child to add to the story by writing sentences using these words.

Challenge
© Harcourt • Grade 1 • Book 5

▶ **Write the word from the box that completes each sentence. You can use a word more than once.**

high	by	Dwight	cried
fly	midnight	night	sky

The Moon Trip

_____   _____

_____ wanted to _____ to the

moon. He was so excited that he jumped out of bed at

_____   _____

_____. "It's time to _____ to the

_____

moon!" he _____. Dwight flapped his wings

_____   _____

and rose up _____ into the _____.

The moon was beautiful! Dwight wished he could stay,

_____

but he had to get home by _____.

 **School–Home Connection**

Challenge

▶ **Use the words in the box to write a story about the picture.**

climbed	Earth	fooling	thought	table

_____

- -

_____

- -

_____

- -

_____

- -

_____

- -

_____

 School–Home Connection

Talk with your child about the picture. Have
your child tell what it might be like to be on a
rocket going to the moon.

 12

Challenge
© Harcourt • Grade 1 • Book 5

▶ **Read the story. Then answer the questions.**

   "This is my big day!" Joan thinks. "I will help Uncle Joe in his bake shop. There is so much to do!"

   "Hurry, Mom!" Joan says. "I can't be late!" She runs down the steps. On the last step, she falls. Her leg hurts.

   "Don't cry," Mom says. "We'll clean your leg. You will be fine."

1. Who is the story about?

_____

- -

_____

2. Where does the story take place?

_____

- -

_____

3. Why is Joan in a hurry?

_____

- -

_____

_____

- -

_____

 **School–Home Connection**

Read the story with your child. Ask your child to tell you what he or she knows about Joan from the story.

13

Challenge

▶ **Complete each sentence. Write the contraction for the two words.**

We   have

_____

- -

1. _____ put on our coats.

_____

you   would

_____

- -

2. If you went out, _____ need a coat.

_____

3. Joan and Ross are not going out.

They   would

_____

- -

_____ rather stay in.

_____

They   are

_____

- -

4. _____ going to come out later.

_____

We   had

_____

- -

5. _____ better go before it gets dark.

Challenge
© Harcourt • Grade 1 • Book 5

Name _____

▶ **Write the word from the box that completes the sentence.**

couch	shouted	out	How
without	town	house	crowd

1. "Dad, we're _____ of milk," Dwight said.

_____

2. Dad said, "I'll go to _____ and get some more."

3. Dwight sat down on the _____ to read. He found something!

4. "Dad!" Dwight _____.

"_____

_____ can you get milk without this?"

 **School–Home Connection**

Have your child read each completed sentence aloud. Together make up a sentence that includes the words *crowd* and *house*. Have your child draw a picture to illustrate it.

16

Challenge
© Harcourt • Grade 1 • Book 5

Name _____

▶ **Read the clues. Then write the words
where they belong in the puzzle.**

blouse	cloud	cow	crowd
flower	growl	house	

1. This is a lot of people.

2. This is kind of a shirt.

3. A tiger does this.

4. This is a plant.

5. This animal lives on a farm.

6. You can live in this.

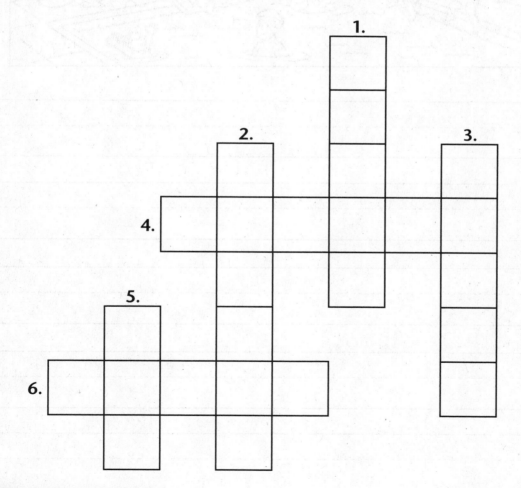

School–Home Connection

Have your child write the words from the box
on a separate sheet of paper. Let him or her
read each clue on this page as you try to guess
the correct word.

18

Name _____

▶ **Use the words in the box to write a
story about the picture.**

answered	baby	heard	pools
done	pushed	together	

_____

- -

_____

- -

_____

- -

_____

- -

_____

- -

_____

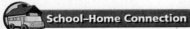 **School–Home Connection**

Have your child read his or her story aloud to
you. Ask your child to describe what he or she
would like to do at a swimming pool.

 19

▶ **Read the story. Answer the questions.**

Mrs. Deer drank some cold river water. She called out, "Little Duke, it is safe. Come and drink." Little Duke was too shy to come out of the woods.

Splash! A catfish called to Little Duke, "Hello! I'm Carl. Fran Frog and I can be your friends."

Little Duke came to the river and had a drink. Soon he and Fran Frog and Carl Catfish were friends.

1. Who is Little Duke?

_____

- -

_____

2. Where does this story happen?

_____

- -

_____

3. What is the story about?

- -

_____

- -

School–Home Connection

Read the story with your child. Ask him or her to describe Little Duke and his new friends and to tell how he or she knows.

20

Challenge
© Harcourt • Grade 1 • Book 5

Name _____

▶ **Write the word from the box that completes the sentence.**

clowns	round	found	frown
ground	downtown	sound	down

The Clown Show

My friends and I went _____ to

see the circus. We _____ good seats.

We sat _____ to see the circus. Two

_____ were on the stage. One had a

smile, and the other had a _____.

They had big, _____ noses. When they

fell on the _____, we all giggled!

School–Home Connection
Have your child read the completed story aloud. Ask him or her to use the word *sound* to write another sentence for the story.

21

Challenge
© Harcourt • Grade 1 • Book 5

Name _____

▶ **Write the word from the box that completes the sentence.**

every	any	stormy	field
happy	worried	sandy	sunny

_____

1. It was a dark and _____ day.

_____

2. Connie was _____ that the sun would never come out.

_____

3. "It's been like this _____ day this week," she said.

_____

4. Then, the rain stopped. It became _____.

_____

5. This made Connie very _____.

 **Try This**

Write a sentence for the word <u>sandy</u>.

School–Home Connection

Have your child read each completed sentence aloud. Together, write a sentence that uses both *any* and *field*.

Challenge

© Harcourt • Grade 1 • Book 5

Name _____

▶ **Write the words from the box that
complete the sentences.**

family	puppy	Lucky	dirty	hungry
soapy	field	Granny	really	

The Lucky Ones

_____   _____

I found a _____ in the _____

_____

beside our house. It was very _____. After

_____

it ate, my _____ took it to a vet. Now the

puppy lives with us. I named my new puppy

_____   _____

_____. My _____ says we're

the lucky ones!

 **School–Home Connection**

Have your child read the completed story
aloud. Ask him or her to use the word *really* to
write another sentence for the story.

25

▶ **Use the words in the box to write a story about the picture.**

great	took	poured	almost
traveled	blue	able	

_____

- -

_____

- -

_____

- -

_____

- -

_____

- -

_____

School–Home Connection

Have your child read his or her story to you. Then talk about other things your child sees in the picture.

Challenge

▶ **Read about Wendy's plans. Then complete the sentences.**

Wendy is planning her birthday party.
"Can my cake have frosting flowers on it?"
she asks Mom.

"Yes," says Mom. "I'll try to get plates with
flowers, too."

"I want to make daisy party hats," Wendy says. She
thinks this will be her best birthday party ever!

1. Wendy wants her cake to have

_____

- -

_____

2. Her mother will try to get

_____

- -

_____

3. Wendy wants to make

_____

- -

_____

School–Home Connection

Ask your child to read the story to you. Invite
him or her to think of another detail to add
that will make Wendy's party more fun.

27

Phonics: Inflections
-ed, -es, -er, -est
(Change *y* to *i*.)
Lesson 28

Name _____

▶ **Add ed, es, er, or est to each word to complete the sentence. Remember that you may have to change the y to i.**

1. Bobby _____ home as it starts to rain.   **hurry**

2. This is the _____ candy I've ever eaten.   **sticky**

3. Dan tells great _____.   **story**

4. Leslie is _____ about something.   **worry**

5. That cat is _____ than my cat.   **fluffy**

🚌 **School–Home Connection**

Have your child read each completed sentence aloud. Ask him or her what happens when each ending is added to the word. (The *y* changes to *i*.)

28

Challenge
© Harcourt • Grade 1 • Book 5

Name _____

▶ **Write the word from the box that completes the sentence.**

| afternoon | zoo | Soon | kangaroo |
| food | new | too | |

My New Friend

_____
- -

. I made a _____ friend at the

_____
- -

_____. I was cold,

_____
- -

and Jenny was, _____.

_____
- -

We hopped like a _____ to get

_____
- -

warm. _____, we were not cold!

School–Home Connection

Have your child read the story aloud. Together, think of some words that rhyme with the words in the box.

30

Challenge
© Harcourt • Grade 1 • Book 5

► **Read the clues. Then write the words from the box where they belong in the puzzles.**

boot	chew	food	goose
grew	hoot	roots	tooth

1. This goes on a foot.

2. This is in your mouth.

3. People eat this.

4. These grow under plants.

5. If you got bigger, you did this.

6. This is a bird.

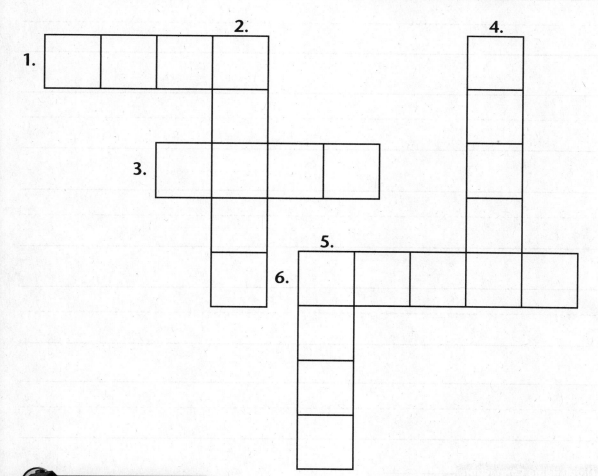

School–Home Connection
Have your child read the clues aloud for you to guess the answers.

32

Challenge
© Harcourt • Grade 1 • Book 5

▶ **Use the words in the box to write a story about the picture.**

boy	building	tomorrow
toward	welcoming	

_____

- -

_____

- -

_____

- -

_____

- -

_____

- -

_____

 School–Home Connection

Ask your child to read his or her story aloud.
Have your child point to the parts of the
picture that fit into the story.

33

▶ **Read the story. Then write some details about it. Use the back of your paper, too.**

Ronnie and his family went to the lake. Ronnie dug holes in the sand while Beth played with the dog. Then they swam in the warm, clear water.

Mom and Dad clapped when Ronnie and Beth did cartwheels in the sand. Then they all flew kites. At the end of the day, Ronnie said, "This is my favorite place! Let's come back again soon!"

_____

_____

_____

_____

_____

School–Home Connection

Have your child read the story to you. Ask him or her to think of details about things people can hear or touch at the beach.

34

▶ **Use a word from the box to make a
contraction that fits the sentence.**

He	can	it	They

The First in Line

The children leave the classroom.

_____

_____ going to lunch.

_____

Lester _____ wait to get to the

_____

lunchroom. _____ first in the line.

_____

_____ like to have a sandwich.

_____

_____ have to get some milk, too.

_____

Now _____ time to go out and play. Lester
is first in the line again!

35

▶ **Write the word from the box that completes the sentence.**

no	find	colt	nobody
tiny	remind	behind	opened

Little Lost Colt

_____

Horse had lost her _____ .

"Oh, _____ !" she cried. "He was

right _____ me." Horse went to

_____ her colt. She asked everyone, but

_____ had seen him. She went back to the

barn to rest. When she _____ the stall

door, her little colt was there waiting!

School–Home Connection

Have your child read the story aloud. Together,
think of words that rhyme with some of the
words in the box.

Challenge
© Harcourt • Grade 1 • Book 5

Name _____

► **Write the word from the box that completes the sentence.**

tidy	robot	won't	kind
Tony	child	behind	bolts

A Helpful Robot

_____ _____

_____ was a smart _____,

_____

but he was always _____ in his chores.

_____

He planned to make a _____ to

_____

_____ his room. Tony drew the

_____

_____ of robot he wanted. "I'll need nuts and

_____

_____," he said, "and two little lights for eyes."

School–Home Connection

Have your child read the story aloud.
Encourage him or her to use a word from
the box to write an ending for the story.

39

Challenge

© Harcourt • Grade 1 • Book 5

► **Use the words in the box to write a
story about the picture.**

any	front	nothing	ready	sorry

_____

- -

_____

- -

_____

- -

_____

- -

_____

- -

_____

 School–Home Connection

Ask your child to read his or her story aloud.
Use words from the box to talk about how the
story relates to the picture.

 40

Challenge
© Harcourt • Grade 1 • Book 5

Name _____

▶ **Put the words in ABC order.**

| zoo | pool | bakery | moon | store | house |

1. _____

2. _____

3. _____

4. _____

5. _____

6. _____

| cave | school | jungle |
| park | town | airport |

1. _____

2. _____

3. _____

4. _____

5. _____

6. _____

School–Home Connection

Ask your child to explain how he or she put the words in order.

41

Challenge
© Harcourt • Grade 1 • Book 5

▶ **Write the word from the box that completes the sentence.**

fold	sold	old	told
gold	hold	cold	bold

Fred and Jim

Fred and Jim were _____ friends. They wanted

to be rich. They went to look for _____. Fred had

_____ his house. "I won't need it," he _____

Jim. They were gone for a long time. One day, it was

very _____. They went into a cave to get warm.

They found gold in the cave! There was so

much gold, they couldn't _____ it all.

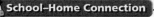
School–Home Connection

Have your child read the story aloud.
Encourage him or her to use a word from the
box to write an ending for the story.

42

Challenge
© Harcourt • Grade 1 • Book 5

Answer Key

Book 1-1

Page 2
1. We have a cat.
2. Pam has a hat.
3. Pat ran to me.
4. She has a bag.
5. We can nap.

Page 4
1. sat
2. hat
3. nap

Page 5
1. Now
2. help
3. Let's

Page 6
1. Accept reasonable responses.
2. Accept reasonable responses.
3. Accept reasonable responses.

Page 7
1. pats
2. tags
3. naps
4. maps
5. bats

Page 9
1. cat
2. can
3. ran
4. mad

Page 11
tan, tap, pat, nap, pan, ant, map, mad, pad, Pam
1. Accept reasonable responses.
2. Accept reasonable responses.

Page 12
1. in
2. no
3. too

Page 13
1. Accept reasonable responses.
2. Accept reasonable responses.

Page 14
bag, jag, rag, sag, tag, wag, hag, lag, nag, band, hand, land, sand

Page 16
1. Kim will sit and dig.
2. It will miss the bin.
3. Tim has six pigs.
4. Jim will give him a mitt.
5. Liz sat to sip the milk.

Page 18
rig, pig, rip, dip, dig, hit, Tim, lit, him
1. pig
2. hit, dig

Page 19
1. soon
2. home
3. so
4. get
5. hold

Page 20
Animals ant, cat, pig, ram
Things mask, van, cap, lamp

Page 21
1. She's
2. There's
3. Here's
4. What's
5. It's

Page 23
1. back
2. sack
3. pick
4. kick

Page 25
1. lick
2. kick
3. sack
4. sick
5. back
6. jacks
7. pack
8. pick

Page 26
1. late
2. Oh
3. Yes

Page 27
2, 1, 3
1. Accept reasonable responses.
2. Accept reasonable responses.
3. Accept reasonable responses.

Page 28
1. Nick ran up a hill.
2. Liz will dig in the sand pit.
3. Yes, it will fit.
4. Jack will fix the mill.
5. The ant bit the fig.

Page 30
1. mop
2. got
3. jogs
4. Bob
5. soft
6. socks

A1

Page 32

mop, Tom, top, pot
got, hog, not, hot

1. mop *or* pot *or* top
2. hog

Page 33

1. much
2. thank
3. find
4. thank

Page 34

Characters Dot, Bob, Mom
Pictures
Accept reasonable responses.

Page 35

1. asked
2. camping
3. added
4. filled
5. handing

Page 37

1. ball
2. wall
3. hall
4. tall
5. call

Page 39

1. mall
2. wall
3. ball
4. tall
5. all

Page 40

1. make
2. Some
3. of
4. how

Page 41

Actions   hop, kick, ran, jog
Names   Bill, Pam, Dan, Rick

Page 42

1. That's
2. can't
3. isn't

4. didn't
5. She's

Book 1-2

Page 2

pet, Ken, best, help, vet, well

Page 4

bet, beg, get, pet, peg
Meg, men, leg, led, gem,
den, gel, Ned

1. pet
2. men *or* leg *or* gem

Page 5

1. time
2. said
3. eat
4. was
5. first

Page 6

1. Accept reasonable responses.
2. Accept reasonable responses.

Page 7

black, bland, blank, block,
blend, bled, blink, blip, blimp,
blond, blot, clamp, clan, clap,
click, clip, clank, clad, clock,
clot, clink, clop, flack, flank,
flap, flick, fleck, flip, flock,
flat, flit, fled, flop, plan, plank,
plop, plot, plod, pled

Page 9

1. The dog gets a bath.
2. Seth and Dan met on the path.
3. The dog is with Beth.
4. This man is thin.
5. Jill picked the fifth doll.

Page 11

1. Beth
2. sixth
3. Then
4. That
5. path

Page 12

1. says
2. water
3. her
4. Mr.
5. new

Page 13

1. camping
2. Sam digs in sand, runs up a hill, hops on a log, and rests on a cot.

Page 14

1. sled
2. slid
3. small
4. still
5. spend

Page 16

hug, gum, mug, bug, hum, hub
bug, rug, tug, but, nut, gut, tub, rub

1. mug *or* bug
2. rug

Page 18

1. cub, tub
2. jug, rug
3. bun, run
4. stuck, duck

Page 19

1. does
2. many
3. food
4. be
5. grow

Page 20

Accept reasonable responses.

Page 21

brick, brag, bran, brass, brim,
crib, crab, crag, cross, crack,
cram, crop, drag, drab, drop,
drum, drip, dress, drug, frog,
from, grab, grass, grim, grip,
grub, Greg, grin, trick, track,
tram, trim, truck, trip, trap

Page 23

Ming, long, wings, swing, ring, song

Page 25

bang, bring, hang, hung, king, long, lung, rang, ring, rung, sang, sing, song, sung, sting, stung, swing, swung, wing

Page 26

1. school
2. use
3. feet *or* head
4. your
5. every
6. way

Page 27

1. He wants to hop.
2. "I can't."
3. Sam and his pals hop. Meg bangs a drum.

Page 28

1. you'll
2. She'll
3. I'll
4. We'll

Page 30

store, for, more, corn, Doris, forget

Page 32

1. for
2. snored
3. morning
4. cord
5. fork
6. more
7. forgot

Page 33

1. animals *or* fish
2. under
3. from
4. very
5. their

Page 34

1. Accept reasonable responses.

2. Accept reasonable responses.

Page 35

1. Response includes backpack.
2. Response includes anthill.
3. Response includes popcorn.

Page 37

fishing, shortcut, catfish, hush, vanish, finished

Page 39

1. shop
2. cash
3. shelf
4. wished
5. finished

Page 40

1. made
2. were
3. Could
4. gold
5. came

Page 41

1. a store; morning
2. a pond; afternoon

Page 42

1. blanket
2. grab
3. skunk
4. clock
5. trumpet
6. slept

Book 1-3

Page 2

1. bunch
2. children
3. catch
4. pitch
5. champs

Page 4

1. Mitch is in the kitchen.
2. He has a sandwich for lunch.
3. There's not much punch left.
4. Mitch checks for milk

Page 5

1. watch
2. air
3. rain
4. grew

Page 6

3, 1, 2

1. Accept reasonable responses.
2. Accept reasonable responses.
3. Accept reasonable responses.

Page 7

mixes, radishes, radish, catches, glasses, glass, catch

Page 9

1. card
2. star
3. yarn
4. mark
5. charming

Page 11

car, farm, far, darling, barnyard, dark, started, arm

Page 12

1. Mrs., house
2. feel, say
3. put, again

Page 13

1. Accept reasonable responses.
2. Accept reasonable responses.

Page 14

1. dusting
2. stacked
3. picks
4. bumped
5. lifting

Page 16
1. Cliff has a quilt on his bed.
2. When will my eggs hatch?
3. Which ball do you want?
4. Ducks quack all day.
5. He whacks the ball hard.

Page 18
1. quick
2. Quinn
3. When
4. Which

Page 19
1. books *or* people
2. read *or* work
3. family
4. writing
5. work *or* writing

Page 20
2, 1, 3
Possible responses are shown.
1. First, the farmer picks the corn.
2. Next, he sells the corn to Mom.
3. Last, we eat the corn.

Page 21
1. popped
2. mopping
3. flapped
4. stopped
5. slipping

Page 23
1. squirrel
2. sir
3. purr
4. fur
5. verse
6. herd

Page 25
bird, perched, chirp, fur, purr

Page 26
1. Cow's
2. nice

3. room
4. always
5. Please

Page 27
1. her new dress
2. hem the dress
3. It is about Hen's new dress that is too big for her.

Page 28
1. taller
2. fresh
3. loudest
4. longer
5. fastest

Page 30
1. pickle
2. pebble
3. shuffle
4. saddle
5. turtle

Page 32
little, uncle, purple, sparkles, cuddle, middle

Page 33
1. buy
2. money
3. other
4. paper
5. carry

Page 34

Main Idea	Many animals live in ponds.
Detail	You can find fish in ponds.
Detail	Frogs hatch from eggs in ponds.
Detail	Some otters live in ponds.

Page 35
1. petting
2. jogged
3. popping
4. stopped
5. planning

Page 37
1. rowboat
2. crow
3. window
4. toad
5. toast
6. elbow
7. soap
8. pillow

Page 39
snow, row, window, moaned, blowing, throw, coat, loaned

Page 40
1. pretty
2. over
3. surprise
4. three

Page 41
Accept reasonable responses.

Page 42
toast, grown, shown, own, thrown, roasted

Book 1-4
Page 2
1. peach
2. Doreen
3. He
4. eagle
5. each
6. clean

Page 4
Possible responses are shown.
bead, beam, bean, beat, beef, beet, deal, Dean, deed, deem, lead, leaf, lean, leash, plead, pleat, read, real, reed, reef, seal, seam, seat, see, seed, seem, seen, sheet, tea, tee, teal, team, teem, teen, she, be

Page 5
Accept reasonable responses.

Page 6
1. Accept reasonable responses.

Page 7
1. You've
2. We're
3. They've
4. You're
5. I've

Page 9
1. Carl and Robert wait for the bus.
2. Jane pays for the popcorn.
3. He may not go out in the rain.
4. The pig eats grain from a bucket.
5. Accept reasonable responses.

Page 11
1. bait
2. May
3. Hooray
4. paid
5. Sunday
6. hallway

Page 12
Accept reasonable responses.

Page 13
A. **What happened?** The boy got wet. **Why did it happen?** It started raining.
B. Accept reasonable responses.

Page 14
trail, fail, jail, mail, maid, pail, paid, rail, raid, tail, snail

Page 16
1. Mom's friend Kate was late.
2. Mom made me wait to eat.
3. Kate came at last.
4. I ate all the food on my plate.

5. Then it was time for the cake.
6. After we ate cake, we played a game.

Page 18
Kate, game, baseball, base, chase, ate

Page 19
Accept reasonable responses.

Page 20
1. Accept reasonable responses.
2. Accept reasonable responses.
3. Accept reasonable responses.

Page 21
plane, Jane, made, grade, Shane, trade

Page 23
1. bites
2. time
3. smiles
4. drive
5. ride

Page 25
1. hive
2. hikes
3. chime
4. nine
5. white
6. pine
7. kite

Page 26
Accept reasonable responses.

Page 27
1. Accept reasonable responses.
2. Accept reasonable responses.
3. Accept reasonable responses.

Page 28
1. baked
2. hiding

3. surprising
4. driving
5. smiling *or* surprised

Page 30
1. dozed
2. chose
3. note
4. rode
5. drove

Page 32
Cole, home, hose, roses, nose, jokes

Page 33
Accept reasonable responses.

Page 34
Possible response: Mark and Seth are best friends.

Page 35
1. bone, hole
2. shone, mole
3. pole, stone

Page 37
1. bridge
2. rice
3. face
4. circle
5. age
6. large

Page 39
pranced, stage, budge, gentle, force, magic

Page 40
Accept reasonable responses.

Page 41
1. lost
2. sick
3. animals

Page 42
1. hasn't
2. She'll
3. doesn't
4. friend's
5. Janet's

Challenge
© Harcourt • Grade 1

Book 1-5

Page 2
1. flute
2. excuse
3. confused
4. mule

Page 4
flute, tune, costumes, used, Luke

Page 5
Accept reasonable responses.

Page 6
Accept reasonable responses.

Page 7
1. chased
2. clapped
3. hoping
4. taking
5. making

Page 9
-ie   pie
        tried
        cried
-y   shy
        my
        myself
-igh   right
        might

Page 11
Dwight, fly, night, fly, cried, high, sky, midnight

Page 12
Accept reasonable responses.

Page 13
1. Joan and Mom.
2. at Joan's house
3. She wants to help her uncle.

Page 14
1. We've
2. you'd
3. They'd
4. They're
5. We'd

Page 16
1. out
2. town
3. couch
4. shouted, How

Page 18
1. crowd
2. blouse
3. growl
4. flower
5. cow
6. house

Page 19
Accept reasonable responses.

Page 20
1. Mrs. Deer's son
2. by a river
3. a little deer who makes new friends

Page 21
downtown, found, down, clowns, frown, round, ground

Page 23
1. stormy
2. worried
3. every
4. sunny
5. happy

Page 25
puppy, field, hungry, family, Lucky, Granny

Page 26
Accept reasonable responses.

Page 27
1. frosting flowers.
2. plates with flowers.
3. daisy party hats.

Page 28
1. hurries
2. stickiest
3. stories
4. worried
5. fluffier

Page 30
new, zoo, too, kangaroo, Soon

Page 32
1. boot
2. tooth
3. food
4. roots
5. grew
6. goose

Page 33
Accept reasonable responses.

Page 34
Accept reasonable responses.

Page 35
They're, can't, He's, He'd, He'll, it's

Page 37
colt, no, behind, find, nobody, opened

Page 39
Tony, child, behind, robot, tidy, kind, bolts

Page 40
Accept reasonable responses.

Page 41
1. bakery   2. house
3. moon   4. pool
5. store   6. zoo
1. airport   2. cave
3. jungle   4. park
5. school   6. town

Page 42
old, gold, sold, told, cold, hold